footlights

Editor: gillian harding-russell
Cover art: Faith Logan
Book and cover design: Tania Wolk, Third Wolf Studio
Printed and bound in Canada at Friesens, Altona, MB

The publisher gratefully acknowledges the support of Creative Saskatchewan, the Canada Council for the Arts and SK Arts.

creative SASKATCHEWAN
Canada Council for the Arts
Conseil des Arts du Canada
sk arts

Library and Archives Canada Cataloguing in Publication

Title: Footlights / by Pearl Pirie.
Names: Pirie, Pearl, author.
Description: Poems.
Identifiers: Canadiana (print) 20200301365 | Canadiana (ebook) 20200301373 | ISBN 9781989274323 (softcover) | ISBN 9781989274330 (PDF)
Classification: LCC PS8631.I78 F66 2020 | DDC C811/.6—dc23

radiant press

Box 33128 Cathedral PO
Regina, SK S4T 7X2
info@radiantpress.ca
www.radiantpress.ca

footlights

PEARL PIRIE

even electricity wants to continue

footlights

for the purposes of night

ample misadventures

pretending there are distinctions

even electricity wants to continue

"Dear Poetry,
It's dark here.
Please hold the light for me.
Yes, just like that."

- John Guzlowski, Twitter

in the room grown dark

there's something that isn't
intention. as surely as anything has atoms
or fields
or vibrations, there's a pressing.

the ears, filled with silence,
want more of what they have.

unplugging the space heater
a blue reaches back as the gap

between plug and outlet increase.
the small, lit flare looks like panic.
it isn't. the arc, completed,
seems like success.

it isn't. it falters at holding the
connection with you

but even electricity
wants to continue.

bath-time lessons

online he narrated the photo
of his 4-year-old in the bath.

she said, 'Daddy, don't put my photo
on the Internet,' but he did.

and as if it were me, my cartoon
avenger self rose to her feet.

sometimes I am covered in triggers.
sometimes I forget I'm a gun.

viral

the glazed gaze. he releases
a watery stool. strangers' feet near
are inconsequential.

he sits in the sun patch, recovering
from gut's tumult.
what signs are illness made of?

across species, you can see youth,
mischief, dominance, and grief &
the universal wobble of the nauseous.

the dishevelled look
an uneven body, tense back,
with posture's limp flail,

unsteady eyes, fewer blinks
pupil's dilation off. in the square
the pigeon looks rough.

*

his level voice asks sombrely
in forced-chipper, *might you*
tear yourself away for a date?

why does his request for attention
harden your busy heart?
you just need to edit 4 more lines.

your face tightens at each
make-sure-it's-audible sob
a few rooms away.

is not distress, distress?
even if your own style
is silent, weeping while you walk?

long game

as the lid on mustard
is burned to rust
by the containment

anger must air,
empty, or else
corrode jaggedly

thru the metal mask
labelled congeniality

aging fast past some tipping point I didn't see

if my skin were any thinner
or drier or more delicate

I'd enter the room with
the hide-dingle of joints

ball and pinion clappers.
the shine is not sweat

but the brassiness
my father called me on–

it finally has its tarnish
knocked off by my ringing.

fingers aren't made only to clasp
each other, folded in a lap but to grasp.

skin wasn't built to bare
for the burden of 'please, listen.'

to slap upside head this hard would be
injurious to hand. to swing the bell,

the heavy weight within, body
rings resonant with Time to Do.

what is set in motion

we paddle the canoe
around the peninsula.

the hill's far shore, as if
on rollers, slides right.

the ripples of skatebugs
disrupts what isn't the moon.

aware of my indelicate
predator eyes,

through its reflection,
I watch the loon.

plumbing

the guest cabin's dimensions
are those of Thoreau's, the boards
and logs, rough hewn.

there is a sink with a tube
to a bucket, plastic keg of water
which forms a modern luck of birth.

spring blossoms white. the diva cup
is full. squatting to pinch it out
it spills into the thirsty floor.

a sin, a repenting. I have made
a blood sacrifice yet feel guilt
more keenly than before.

I scrub but it's absorbed. I pour
water. the water stains, worse,
watermarks a ripple in the grain.

the tree still feels the season–
spring bursts a bead of sap
from cut limbs, immortal pine.

an ant by lamplight

she has been zipping
        her third circuit
                of the lampshade's rim

pausing, head tilted.
        we, despite ourselves,
                cheer. she's started down:

antennae flicking,
        she veers, pauses
                backtracks to the rim

reversing course
        one loop, another
                bopping the same loose

thread of the shade, third—
        hers are our tiny black feet.
                we can't help ourselves.

in the night window
        I catch the eye of
                my own laughing face.

the large black ant
        should forage the table.
                we, *deus ex machina,*

tap the littlest one down,
        our own heroism questionable
                expect her uninjured, better.

let us make

myths of ourselves instead of the usual
fools. let's see those teeth

of bluegrass blade. each one is a particular
that will not return to this light.

we can pour every love on this grass,
each sensation, funk, love, and ache. they

are only things to walk among, attached
as shadows are. as outcomes of conditions.

let us not karate each other awake
with questions but marvel us.

to get all we desire

ask for it, rain to out-tick
all the clocks

I pray this to no god
in particular

all ground is holy. to stand here
is my prayer on this land.

to pause is to work out
what remains

to make satisfaction
complete.

friends

for B, r & S

"...those crevices of silence
wedged between flight and sound..."
– "To My Friends," by Wisława Symborska

stand closer
don't keep this
polite fissure —
moss takes years

ferns, bluebells
poplar trees and pines
will bridge this space
between our pelvises —

press in with the weight
of your attention —
collapse towards me
one point of hip,
then the other

rest with me,
shoulders-stable, lean.
let's make of us
a hibernaculum
for snakes to find.

sleeping with head injuries

the chair's back is more straight than
mine, my head-heavy spine droops.

his road burn looks like a rash
scraped under the forearm's skin.

in ICU the world is pump swish
quiet with rainbow vials for blood.

I want to photograph those hands
between nurses and neurologists –

you say it's uncouth somehow.
those hands, black ground into them

dirt under the nails, long and ragged
from working baler twine and wire.

on the sly I photograph tourniquets,
number-machines, creating patterns.

next time I watch the sleeping hands.
they have thinned, been scrubbed,

nails trimmed, wrist cool to the touch
rough hacks moisturized out or healed.

all of the arthritis disappeared in weeks
of not pushing, Sisyphus against pain.

fine, smooth, whitened glove-palms
of a gentleman, like his own father's.

in a state of reception

brackets for steps
extension cord
metal metric screws
asphalt shingles
deck screws
waiting for the list
to become a poem
and enlighten me.

neighbours

the flyer is a tumbleweed of waste, excess
inequity and greed, to catch against our brick needs.

a neighbour screams, pottery against their wall.
Syria has scuds, Brazil, arsonists. my aunt

has lost her husband, my cousins, their dad.
the wind and rain get down my collar.

rain brings encouragement to mycelium
and aches to my stubbed broken toe.

Albrecht Dürer's *Linden Tree* lifts—
huh, this painting has always had sound.

with a thundercloud of juvenile grackles
dispersed, the tree looks, impossibly, the same.

we fear we, too, are unchanged
despite the goosebumps, the vows, the quiet.

considering the shuttle

for mini-wheat's loom
speculating on reasons
that cereal boxes
don't credit photographers

and whether
I should practice my French
via *riboflavine, folate...*

considering the sensation
of a poem's release
into words, the work
of a toothpick
at popcorn kernel
stuck between teeth

considering how belief and truth
and flowstate are all sensations and
how sugar, insomnia, mania, and caffeine
boost the sensation of clarity
but not the fact.

weed trees want all the sun

"Life is the default."
– Clark Blaise in *The Meagre Tarmac*

Manitoba Maples have a desperation
matching my own.

the row of dead stumps, and stunted attempts
age like Scottish eyebrows—

they twist into the chain-link, awaken
their small flags of green, their refusals to surrender

are we not most like those
whom we won't understand?

the ligaments hop over each other

here, put your thumbs
(each deserve an Order of Canada)
into my waiting shoulders,
into the scoops
along the spine, into tension
into the filet mignon of my aching.

footlights

"If you ever find yourself in the wrong story, leave."
- Mo Willems in *Goldilocks and the Three Dinosaurs*

in the wings

"wings, detach. break free."
– rob mclennan in *distinctions*

sometimes walking is more of a miracle
than a woman in flight. take up your wings
from the ground and walk at any pace.
by walk I mean go any place.

interstitial sidewalks are a risk. boys
and women with masking tape take turns, independent
of each other. independent thinking, they think.

attach paper wings. they were never your wings.
were never really wings; no muscle.

you have muscle you will not lend to this.
be as delicate with the day as with
the pincushion-lonely: what you say will echo
as the only, will get more

importance than a word stranded alone on a line,
and more weight than it merits.
hush your needled self
until at least you've felt the warmth of a shower.

the daylight is eager to see you
but don't hold that against it.

some gifts flatter. some pin.
none we are not obliged to keep.
the gift is
wanting to give, exchange, lift.

each step away is also a lifting self up.
choose each step towards.
what matters is what happens next.

the saplings are yellow as footlights in the forest

how to deny the season
when stoking a wood fire.
the foot is forgetting sandals
while, beside the thumbs,
paddle-callouses thin.

father's birthday is a week past.
a gaze at the calendar
lowers without a word.
then I should say: clouds moved
across the sun smoothing away
any harsh shadows, then night
swallowed evening's curves.

but that would be too tidy
and outside, drizzle and sun
collects in the shallow scoop
of the garden shovel again.
time to go out, rinse and dry
care for mood as I would my tool.

woodpile

chill gathers at the same time of day
makes me look up at the stack beside the stove.

each time the white sun hovers its smudge
two fingers above the horizon.

to cut and to burn are sister acts,
a destruction and a survival of cold.

I've split enough kindling when
the hand-shaped hickory snaps.

the maul handle's label is a medic alert bracelet
that reads: 3-5 pound capacity. it's serious.

I put a 6 pound head on it, briefly. no fair or foul,
sometimes, when a head rolls, it's not mine.

bless

for years I would inherit the earth
but I'm no longer meek enough

to nod, receive the destruction,
the stripped & the desecrated.

oaks continue to drop acorns.
pupating in cotton & predawn light

dubbing his dick move a teapot
does nothing towards a cup of tea.

so he brags of being a bastard...
what right have I to override

his sense of self? acorns drop.
those who consume them will.

all eyes up here

scuba in beer breath. deep-sea life up close—
his flushed bow and arm pump at applause.

what's it like to be proud and sure
as a young man at an open mic?

in break watch how he grabs from midair
someone's call, 'Great poem'.

that wasn't lobbed his way.
he doesn't look up, says thanks,

smiles at the credit due. he's already
working on his next rhymed opus.

he never assumes he didn't kill it.
writes of his ex thru the opener

goes home before the feature,
confident the world's eating him up.

schmooze king

if name-dropping were an education, I'd have my
PhD in hand by the time I closed that door, firmly

then sprinted until blood was forced from its loops in amygdala
of insult to the insula and scattered into a full-frontal confetti laughter.

Let it bloody pour, let's joke until dry riverbeds dive under lakes
for cover, and I swim deaf. humming will burst from every surface.

at the gardening centre

Lady With The Badge didn't answer
but proffered a pamphlet on native species
with held breath

which junipers
are male or female?

she rolled her eyes as if
she won't hear that,
as if I'd asked if her pantyline
were pride of dignity, proof that she isn't
the kind to go without.
such a set of jaws
is a dentist's profit

sometimes *I don't know* is a phrase of shame.
maybe she's new, afraid of being exposed
as ignorant. maybe her brain explodes
like mint rhizomes at the complexity of her day
maybe no one sells female because
cities hate fruit.

my trolley cart of ferns
squeaks on left turns.
lines everywhere, queues to choose—

the door of birdsong

in a few months this sliding glass
will have a cross-section of ice crusts.

I hold this screened breeze and
accept I'll let go of the good.

a field cricket kicks
his pulse in my palm.

the cat is running, a jaguar
scaled for moths.

is it stoicism to be prepared
to dig the darling's grave

or depression's eye-slits
in feathered masquerade?

as if leaving a movie, blink to
these hundreds of greens.

what follows

I dreamt McDs Happy Meals
had packs of Canadian poet trading cards.

my get-up-and-go must have.
it isn't here.

the cat proves she's understudied ravens
whenever the bathroom steams.

a fast, hot shower in a cold room
could be poverty, or a Nordic spa.

sunburn's socks can't be taken off.
applause responds to applause as itch to scratch.

applesauce is responded to
by sore throats and cat mews.

just say you had a healthy baby.
don't declare a gender. some girls have penises.

even lemmings aren't as we thought but
people follow fascists because they lead.

the 'derelict house' now has Christmas lights.
standard presentation isn't standard.

if a few of us survive, our successors
will have as much to do as we do.

for the purposes of night

"You're making your problem,
everyone's problem.
Fix it silently."

–Michelle Richardson to her Grade 3/4 class

lifting for the purposes of night

the moon's face is both up
and downwards.

in incandescence a
glossy-leafed houseplant

feels how the bottom
of an airplane wing

lifts. night sky slips
the room into bluer.

night suggests, anything
could happen.

a mosquito rides
the cross-ventilation.

momsense

between singing ‘I love my Oscar Mayer Weiner,’
and Sesame Street’s segment on how to make bannock

the mother said, your father wants more kids.
I say I am trying, but I got an IUD.

it’s a little wire that means I can’t get pregnant.
don’t tell your father. it’s a secret.

age-inappropriate sharing, even a child knew that much
but what mother doesn’t need a friend?

*

sitting on the cement door stoop the mother plucked grass
and said she’d teach her daughter to play music.

find a blade like this, with teeth on it, rough
and hold it like this between your thumbs and blow.

they played for a while then she plucked
a wild Geranium and asked, you know what this is?

it’s champagne weed. do you know why they call it that?
because they make champagne from it to destroy people’s
lives.

*

as the eggbeater spun
the girl snuck a finger into the batter

her mom said, you know when I
was your age I was making a cake with a friend

and she stuck her tongue
in the bowl. the eggbeater hit it.

wide-eyed the girl asked what happened

this!

the mother said sticking out her cupped tongue—
the girl screamed, fell off the stool.

what used to work with me

"I'm not going to censor myself
to comfort your ignorance."
–Jon Stewart, comedian

it's only fair to warn you: the buttons you've known,
have changed. I've land-mined them. cow eyes explode.

when you hear yourself think, he ain't that pretty
admit it, you're a terrible but well-meaning liar.

the highest honour is to minimum sufficient force.
this is, unequivocally, nope, not happening.

deafness has its advantages. twist a small dial.
more natterings go away, if slapped.

he holds my eye in a game of chicken then
lets me off the look. I stumble as if shoved

but it's all good. no cattle were harmed
in the making of these statements.

if you hold a stumble

by the corner of its photo
the awkward ankle-twist
about to happen, loops, loops.

the fall never completes
nor is it released to a flattering
recovery, and grace of stride.

the caught breath of
shift, the latch of gasp
is a captive of the page

we self-imprison
by watching the careen. for life
let us move off the paper.

pollinators think the bouquet is for them

the yellow rivet
of the daisy is
made of flowers
all the way down
to the green cup
that formed for
its own sake.

readying crudities

under the flared cone of a porch lamp,
white knuckles of cauliflower and the couple
sit duel-bodied as greedy prayers over the rushed hearts.

thru nostril-flared hosannas, bitterness grows a rose garden
of stars. they turned, bruised, *aimoforo angeío*
as if they were angels fighting each other for sun

then flopped exhausted in the shade. an almond milk toast:
to woman and to food. another to the silt *éclectique*
and to the *kókkalo* of the hammer in our ears.

it's all the leisure and no weeding when you grow anger
that overgrows all. only comets pass hotter. they too return.
there's a pattern if you make all the observations,
selectively enough, impartially enough, for long enough.

highway

"All spaces are political spaces."
—Natalie Hanna, on Facebook

points for carrying flares in his truck
points for not too much damage
on the grill nor to the guardrail
points for walking away
points for someone stopping
how many point buck, neck-twisted
points for all the skid marks
that might have been enough.

listening for

the Hereford stands apart
from the stones & her fellows,
shivers off flies.

her forehead's white curls
press the hydro pole as if
she could concentrate and
pick up a voice she once knew.

under the yard light the farmer
considers mercy killing. a sparrow
hit the glass. broken neck or stunned.

he can't stand to let a creature suffer
for he's a decent man, claims
wet lashes of the cow,
when her calf is sold, is from wind.

he explains how she behaves
how cows all became, not
losing hope, but forgetting their calves

all is a quiver
which you notice
or you ignore.

see how a dog
removes tremble of nerves
with a shake

or a concerned man
with profundo vibration
props his steeple-hands against
the wooden air.

in stillness the inner eye
watches their performances
while intestines quake.

the forest behind

thickened with me
until I was 10, then it
became a woodlot.

I aged. the standing trees
became younger
on average, thinner.

some matured. a few… one oak
was left alone because
a wire fence grew through it.

the barbed wire these years
embedded in me
prevents a casual killing.

living memory closed
its bark over seamlessly.
some fool who tries, dies–

the kickback of chainsaw
would catch on my metal.
that cut would heal too.

claustrophobia

"The ocean doesn't exist for my mother's cat.
It lives in a world three stories high
and thinks that going down into the cellar
is going outside."
– "Finite Flight" by Colleen Redman

shooed out, Cheryl can see only bright past her squint.
at ten she sees potential where peers see games: the choke-hold
of jump rope, how Dad's razor has removable blades.

has anyone told her about her uncle's youth, when discipline
meant being pulled out of sleep, harangued in a locked hall closet,
no crack of moon, bangs on the door to keep him awake for days.

how he grew to use his father's back to crack open drywall.
she's slapped for touching the thermostat, blamed for making them
all bankrupt. uncle needs the open road, no confines.

in winter his windows are opened for air. in summer's stifle
Cheryl needs the shade of a book. she'd rather be a bookworm
than reply too boldly, would rather be eaten by worms.

lost in a very small maze

my resolve is to solve her public
smile. stemmed from his shoulder clap
her pat has a thumb dug in as a warning.

much is in the spin. my axle is mercy,
dizzying mercy. feeling a drop run
down my leg I think blood. sweat, I think.
my unconscious has been leaking again.

even when he doesn't look
the looking away is as much of a telltale.
yet he would blindfold her too.

if looks could melt steel, a molten river.
her claim staked. her beefcake.
who I would nourish, protect behind my gates?
her from herself, or him from *her*?

as the tops die

grey is not the season for eyes
but for hands, tongues.
under overcast skies
cup from the frost-wet earth
potatoes. wash, scrub
boil them until their skins
slip loose. add milk, mash
eat and still they taste dry
as a mouth in the morning.
they and I are unquenchable.

most days

I seem to wear purple or grey
as one big mobile bruise

a corner of a nail snags
keeps drawing attention

once clipped it is
a tiny moon, dropped, lost

like harsh words from childhood
once we hear behind them

where they were coming from
once all the feels have faded.

there are larger things.
as of October 2018

there are 3,851 confirmed planets
spinning in 2,871 systems.

as of November 2019, there are
4,000 confirmed exoplanets in the Milky Way.

here, ecosystems collapse: insect,
coral, bird, tree populations all plummet.

some point to mythical Quebec values
as if not immigrants, on indigenous land

one white dude shoots seniors
because he thinks Jewish prayer is a risk

more than his own small
septic catchment of existence.

waiting for menus

a pigeon collides with the end wall
of Pho Ba Ga King
the rest of the flock veered clear.

a new shape appears
over the red awning.
there's a mid-air spiral of 4 wings

a blush-breasted hawk
has the klutz in talons.
for minutes the Cooper's hawk

watches traffic
standing on her chest
feet casually squeezing.

I write item #54 on the order slip,
anticipate a warm, full belly
look up and the awning is empty.

ample misadventures

"Laughter saves lives."
—Asia Barclay in chat

the bigger small questions

at Chapters (I know, sorry) I asked
a clerk where the poetry was. she
flubbed off: poetry is everywhere. Dear
Sweet Lady. That's Not Useful for my Question.

your chaste triage fills my puppy gaze.
I compare you to a sanctuary. your
polka dots of skulls are a fabric we
could dance to. but not right now. direct
me to the geese migrating north–
all these high rises, lights and signs addle.

like me, and the oldest species on earth
we can't leave soon enough. shadows point
everywhere from fluorescent bulbs, confused
they can't bloom. the slats around compost, rot.

homogenized script

for Gladys and Joy & their *Watchtowers*

what if the universe isn't moral?
what if most people are not, in fact, lost?

crab apples fall to the street, attract wasps
ants. nothing in the system can be gone-gone.

even the young men assigned to my door
are somewhere in their tidy ties and suits,

those to whom I opened for the knock
while on the phone with open bathrobe

giving them a show, leading to Joy
and Gladys' assignment to my district.

my good apple-cheeked women.
there is no soul. body and mind go.

religion would pasteurize you,
all the complexity of one fruit removed

by mixing you with the whole harvest as juice.
as you strain yourself, are poured

gelatine-firm and glowing red in rows
straight-sided jars, unopened,

a jelly against the long cabbage winter.
the beauty of faith is undeniable.

I don't like them apples to be bruised,
I take their tract, match their salesman smile.

in the park's verges

dark evening grass proves it.
as fog on a grape is rubbed away
you are shiny now. once, none of you

had skin-brushed gloss. you are a cosmos.
you are bright as my insides,
as this swallowed sun of my entrails.

dim spots are cloth and missed spots
that need my lips. where I have touched glows.
closed-toe sandals make nipples of your toenails,

under the slats of leather, the little piggies wink.
they have the density of fireflies between blinks.
rays shoot out as you reach inside your shirt

to scratch the many suns of your chest.
will our ribs find they can intermesh like fingers
in a bit of scrub and cedar verge?

I could show my glow but inching past your body,
pointing to Helleborine, I cloud you.
your back arches a stretch, flashes your waist

flashlight handprints where my palms lingered
one beat, two beats, tens of beats.
our feet are less light, less lit than faces.

mistaking a trashed straw for a hope of
a Hairy Pinesap, we're off the gravel path.
against the poplar's smooth bark your light is cast.

these trees so young none believe their smooth bark
will brindle, find its cantaloupe rind. none believe
they will be enclosed in ropes, lumbered off

when the expansion into home comes close.
bark on bark on bark and our footfalls press.

closer is pine and is pine and is pine-needles' red

a softening sound. there is the hollow pit as you swat
a bug from your back, a nervous grooming.
under your shoulder blade is a shallow cave.

a moonlit fox heavy with almost birth might
leave the mole hunt. she waits. mistakes you
for a safe culvert. the hunting is rich.

the hidden soft and firmer where my arms
have trailed off, hugs slipping down
like your shirt might. it surprises, the leaning.

the thin musk of your pores, your neck,
the bristles my cheek knows briefly. the dark
of your expression, an uncertain withdrawal,

the puzzle of your humidity that aches light.
I feel the strain in my back. will you put more good
in goodbye when you next step backwards?

adaptive

it makes sense that a pear bruises.
its biggest bump used to be the ground
for seeds to release. now analogy fails.

mammals don't sprout from broken ribs.
injury has its own lessons.
it says: wrap yourself in soft cotton.

it says: be gentler than your habit.
watch for those who may pile on
canned answers, solutions.

as we heal, let's breathe
incant how we ascend past biology,
we're breeze, hornet and stem in able tension.

all in

like dough
in a bread pan.

I rest, rise.
it snows and sleets.

so. we live
north of warm.

I thank this bed
these sheets

the quiet of
grey scale night.

prayer moves
nothing but

the warm mouth.
lips licked,

a small inhale
of cool-air words,

the sensation
of pre-kiss.

old habits are hard as a boiled egg to beat

I learned to waltz from Mom
who learned to waltz from Dad.

she learned to dance by following
so she taught me to dance the lead.

later those kitchen radio nights made
for awkward wrestles with the beau.

some steps you learn are more than
you'll ever need; it's power to know.

the child's geared up

purple glitter rubber boots, pink-caped rain slicker,
and batman umbrella.

—walk is a go. I repeat walk is a go.
—roger that, Parent 1.

let's promenade a babble thru puddles, chins up
sweat wets bangs, colour saturates

as sun—
until steps lag. (do we lug her home?)

"uncle" is something big people say. kids
don't give up. not a baby anymore.

a flannelette's flannel

for a long winter's night with an owl
and owlet, a light: a triolet and a trio

of delight: a booklet and books
set aside for mending. a coverlet's cover

of thread, blinked eyelets and eyes,
a tablet, a tab, an outlet, an out.

a couplet and a coup, a doublet and almost
doubt for the bullet's bull.

a violet viol's small tune.
a bracelet, a brace, a chalet, and a chal

a shan't and a pamphlet's own pamph,
slight burn. and a sobri's own coal sobriquet.

pinned to our heels

let's spin our shadows, long donkey's tails
pinned on each of us

I love two hours before sunset
for its reversals.

the limp hydro wires
reflect as if white.

at night driving up Kanata's hill
Ottawa is a fallen starfield

and our collective petty sparks usurp
the glory of sky.

before you smell ozone

blue jay jaws are propped open
with a racket—

cows shift and sniff.
a storm's coming—

even your knees know
surely as the dog's hackles stand.

'away' is the only direction the dog finds
for her eyes.

the German Shepherd pulls tight
on the chain clipped to her collar

she's at the end, but not the only end.
there's a range of slack that we've forgotten.

shake them wasps out of your shoes.
before you smell ozone, move.

ample misadventures

sit down. a migraine is a signal,
not a bat signal. the pain pin's directive:
we're vulnerable, hide until this passes.

peak sensitivity to light implores: away,
away, you gnome. nausea commands: curl.
the crux of all survival is self-defence.

even a pulled green onion knows enough
to makes a husk from outer leaves
to ensure moist interiors are safe.

so too a dry remark keeps blades at bay
so no nick will open doors for mould
to rot the wet electric body within.

the body wisdom believes its own
distress. its healing magic is not quick.
it's a stopgap, a whisper networks. listen.

pretending there are distinctions

Me: "I would like one easy day.
Do you suppose one is back-ordered?"

Her: "No, ma'am. Tomorrow
should be a challenge too."

each against the other

the stretch of green twigs
from the maple limb

against the power line is
an instrument of storm.

this bowstring makes home
into a 2x4 framed resonator,

a drone against sky.
the bucksaw in hand.

from memory, feverfew tea's
straw scent: my teenage pout

the heaviest hay bales
left for my mother.

a summer concert's brought
to an end. sawdust in the eye.

your beard has become
my fur fortress. hold me.

honey locusts shed gold at whippet dawn

along the cracked sidewalks
dog, bright as a mote
translucent as a glass fish.

why should I remark on him?
you all say, everything has to be some
way. that is his.

not a glance towards us, the dog lopes
towards home, away from mine
of carved mossed stone.

a root knowing

the sodden weight of cardboard, the
squiggle of garden hose, and the hammer
are equal impediment to crabgrass.

wide or narrow, able to rot in months
or rust over millennia, the grass
doesn't distinguish. its business is itself.

all it knows is its own immediate crack of
more bright that way, how it must push
shoots across, along, thin, white, enough,

borrow from its saved energy, borrow
from the parts that have made it out
green, and grow past that which blocks.
it does no good to think. it needs.

house with you

you would make a wonderful wingchair
my back to your stomach, your jaw for my temple

you as accent colour, a wall to catch the eye. fuzzy chin
a cushion to wrap around, spiral my octopus self…

you're so serious, yes, dignified. I might take you as a desk
placed near a window where you'll absorb morning sun

have you heard of the Japanese art of nantaimori?
your glass chest made for a bed tray of sushi…

or you, I could see you as a floor lamp,
that glow of your eyes has no dimmer.

Helena relates the scene at the pub

(Tewt's pan pipes shrilly play. a scamper
of bacchanalian hooves. I look from the doorway.)

lo, what softness in his eyes, iron in his thighs;
virtue in his heart, fire in every part of

the dibs-claimed man. Mighty Herculean ring,
the fist he props under his honest chin.

with flirts subtler than a younger man
with the tone spike of have a *girl*friend

I'm mentioned like the incidental zap-bump of
knee, the reflexive pretzeled legs, yogic arms.

force of habit blushes, expects sin and blame.
she leans her frame for ego-massage, not a score.

note the accidental charms of his shoulders as
they strain, squirm, turn towards the door.

-*you afraid, Herc?* asks sidekick Newt.
-*I need silence, Newton; let me think.*

get thee behind me, Dydo.
still she persists, and teases my man.

that New Year's party we had

when, for every person who said No,
or Maybe, I invited someone else

but on the night, maybes and nos
came and brought friends and
there must have been 60 people
in our 1-bedroom apartment.
at 2 a.m. we wanted everyone to go.
knots were still deep in discussion—

it was like that between us but for
an afternoon and it was words
that would not relent, stories I swear
I didn't tell. emptied, the next day I slept.

measuring the day's ring size

"The everyday is the most important day."
—*Ikea Catalogue* (2015)

an outboard in a water trough
diy-Jacuzzi would be less distracting
than your music

like a morning glory at dusk
my posture curls shut as
the evening comes.

I can't distinguish exercise
the cardio rise from the amp up
of panic attack's thrust

you don't feel like
scalloped potatoes?
are you too rich to be given wealth?

for safety, we must move
to where bombs fall so threat is palpable
not swayed by microns of moods

as worn thin as nerves are by missiles
people can be optimistic
because they must.

that's false, huh. destruction and hate
does not concentrate a soul's salt.
being jumped doesn't equate to no down days.

your blanket treatment is kind:
love is not a reward we make
and give, for lack of mistakes.

some days we wake with threat
in the chest, and some days
are gentle as your voice of concern.

absent-mindedness is my stairmaster

the white noise of a suburb is my guru.
wind that picks fruit is my caffeine
and small ink marks are my food.

take the clean towels upstairs to fold, two
per drawer, come down with them still
on the arm, holding plates, book and spoon.

books are my friends, and yours too,
Mom said, my mind can't shut off without
reading for hours into the gloom.

Chinese thumb traps, cough suppressant, flu.
Mom and I read our books and write them,
watch weather rain, as it must.

you can't plant a carrot

in a ruby and water it with diamonds or
pixels. no emerald ever brought forth a tree.
stasis brings no urge to eat or grow.

you can't fruit friendships on rarity.
the dirt, with its weeds and diseases
reaches deep beneath digital pace.

we need sloppy mud, bugs, and failures
of sun, not a loupe and clever skill
to seed moments, sprout, regrow.

at the Experimental Farm where M. lived

for golden hour, our youth is given back.
we are a flock of starlings to brabble the snow.

the route should have landed them here
when there was ample food. but no.

straight ahead is the darkest. the horizon behind
has the sunset to warm shoulders.

no, I don't know the new or what's for supper
but snow geese land in corn stubble.

your neck is feathery, my wings block
any wind that would bite you.

speeds of ephemerality on Bronson St.

the bakery has been replaced
with a Tae Kwon Do studio.

not all signifies as lichen does
on this fissured heart–

a warm breeze hovers on breasts
almost like a nuzzled kiss.

dust

"Everything's mine but just on loan."
–"Travel Elegy," by Wis□awa Szymborska

it's impossible not to own
something. a worry stone
cloistered in sweat, the tip
of your nose even if it looks
like mother's. what you hold
with your eyes: the roll of hills
on this dawn, alone, the presidency?

all eyes have the power to say mine
when fire, water, drought
war and death have taken all
or when all is fine enough.
look, some speck of desire for good
inside is unshared but not
unreachable. any mote in clouds
may be the nucleus of a flood.

humming is how humans purr

"The moss wants the snow that the stone does not."
–Kevin Matthews, Instagram

the warm body of earth
melts the snow as it lands

except on the culvert
where the air beneath is warmer,

and on oak leaves, insulation enough
to keep the snow intact

and on your hood which reflects
the colour of your eyes

a coniferous rim of green
around a heated pool.

vacant lot beside IGA

bent in fluorescent nausea, scent headache.
the only dangerous chemtrails are in aisle 8.

brain fog lost a dialogue with Interact
and 3 strike passwords. too late.

quick break. about to fly apart
like a beaded necklace

the clerk with clear gaze commiserates
with bunching around her eyes –

hers, the only human contact for days.
apart from averted gazes.

some can only see as far as the dangerous side.
whatever snaps your shutter, eh.

see the smallest beetle on the stem of chicory
the dew beads on the palmed leaf going nowhere.

step into a choir loft of crown-tipped coral mushrooms.
put a macro between the hairs of a bumble bee's leg.

a stranger's body built of fury and mud
is nothing I can solve. not all is my job.

Acknowledgements

Gratitude towards gillian who helped me see what was here.
Thanks to all who touch base and encourage, weigh in on poems.
You know who you are.

Previous versions of these poems have appeared in the following:

"adaptive," *The New Quarterly,* (Spring 2020).

"after the wake," *Saltstains* (Haiku Canada, 2016).

"aging fast past some tipping point I didn't see" and "in the room grown dark," *Poemeleon,* ed. by rob mclennan, (The Canadian Issue, 2018).

"bath-time lessons," a flutterbook (TerryAnn Carter, 2013).

"each against each other"

"friend," a limited-run, birchbark broadside (2014).

"Helena relates," above/ground broadside #287 (March, 2009). *The Mighty Hercules.* Dir. by Joe Oriolo Trans-Lux Television, 1963. Animated Series.

"let us make," above/ground broadside #320 (August, 2013).

"neighbours," after *Linden Tree on a Bastion,* and "weed trees want all the sun," *Trail & Landscape,* ed., Annie Bélair, Vol. 53, No, 4, October-December issue (*Ottawa Field Naturalists,* 2019).

"plumbing," *Gush: Menstrual Manifestos for our Times,* eds. Ariel Gordon, Rosanna Deerchild, and Tanis MacDonald (Frontenac House, 2018).

"readying crudities," *Canthius* (Issue 7, fall 2019).

"Sleeping with Head Injuries," *Big Smoke Poetry,* eds. Steve Meagher and Daniel Meaghe, issue 5 (January, 2018).

"to get all we desire," rout/e, broadside (CS Art project, Sept 2016) and as a chapbook, *rout/e* ed. Chris Turnbull (2017).

"waiting for menus," *The New Quarterly,* (Spring 2020).

"woodpile," a finalist in the Paterson Poetry Contest (May 2018).

Pearl Pirie is a queer concussed writer living in rural Quebec. Her poetry collection, *the pet radish, shrunken* (Book*hug, 2015) won the Archibald Lampman Award. Her manuscript *Thirsts* won the Robert Kroetsch Award for Innovative Poetry and was published in 2011. Her first trade collection was *been shed bore* (Chaudiere Books, 2010). Her poems have been included in *Best Canadian Poetry in English* twice, and have appeared in various anthologies. Her newest chapbooks are *Call Down the Walls* (Frog Hollow Press, 2019), *Eldon, letters* (above/ground, 2019), *Not Quite Dawn* (Éditions des petits nuages, 2020) and forthcoming, Water loves its bridges: *Letters to the dead* (The Alfred Gustav Press, 2020). She runs phafours press, Chalkpaths manuscript editing service, and Studio Nouveau workshops. Pearl lives in Wakefield, Quebec.